Father and Sun

By Bernard M. VanSluytman &
Darius J. VanSluytman

Paperback ISBN: 978-0-578-21973-8

Cover design: D. VanSluytman
Photos: B. VanSluytman
Layout: D. VanSluytman
Edited: Gail VanSluytman & Ayanna VanSluytman
(this project is truly a family affair)
Printed in The United States of America

Published By: Island Lifestyle Group LLC
Winston-Salem, NC

Dedication (BMV)

To my family, wife and children: My love has always been the jazz, never the blues.

Acknowledgment

We acknowledge family and friends who helped us along our path, anciently and presently:

Generations of family (VanSluytman, Cummings, Davis, Fernandes, Johnson) who withstood the ignominy of the lash, promise of freedom and braved the new world.

Virgin Islands friends: The Hodge Family (Ms. Dolly, Mr. Ed, Stedman, Larry, Maria, Verne), the late Hon. Alexander Farrelly, Governor, The Family of the late John de Jongh, Esq., The Roberts Family, Teddy and Angela Bryan, and family, The Family of Rudy Slack, The Recaldo Lettsome Family, Mary Alexis Rhymer, Lemuel Callwood ESQ, and the late Llewellyn "Big Lew" Sewer.

*Work denoted BMV by Bernard M. VanSluytman, work denoted DJV by Darius Jamal VanSluytman

Table of Contents

Music, Man!

Drum beats recall
Ancient, distant tongues,
Translations unwritten. Forgotten.
But syncopation and rhythm
lends understanding
if listened.

Meanings hard written into our very soul, our DNA

Jazz, Calypso, Reggae, Hip Hop, Rhythm and Blues
Stubborn resistance to cultural destruction of ebony hue.

Music, man! Armor against extinction of a people and their art.

BMV

SCATTERED REMNANTS

... and so I watch visitors and residents alike
nestle and melt into alabaster sand
oblivious of the crushed sea shells and
remnants of ancestors into which they sink.
Sands scattered by the weight of ages, sun, sea, storm
and the evil of man.

The spirits of ancestors watch without comment or judgment.
Except every now and then you can hear an angry, impatient
low trade wind moan, praying for a time as it was in the beginning.
man in God-colored hue
man loved of old,
man loved anew.

BMV

Pieces of El Dorado Gold

He whistled going and coming
and marveled at the cruelty of man
said to be made in the image of a higher being

He laughed in a manner of a screech like
a colorful bird of the forest or savannah
and drank rum neat chased with water

Mouth organ or guitar in hand
He was a one-man band
and would fall asleep comfortably
in the embrace of trust surrounded by wife, family, friends.

Compay, his old countrymen called him.

Never a man of words, he taught by slow, steady action
his children learned to understand the importance of time,
education, work steady in order to prevail.

Such from a Guyanese countryman, in NYC,
Who never completed 4th Standard.

He cooked for others.
Our mother cooked for us.

She, loving and forgiving, but
mistrustful of white power

she, daughter of foreign soil, would not say, but
could not forget, the brilliant lie and tyranny that was "Great"
Britain, and the affront, the indignities visited by the US on
its sun-ripe citizens of her hue. So she would not work for dem so.
Not she, meh chile. But it was fear disguised in bravado and tough
chat.

So she, a lady of 6th Standard education, labored for us, not them.
So she thought!

We cope the best we can in a foreign land of anger, brutality and
mistrust of its own creation.

Her logic came at us in a lilting Guyanese dialect about education,
self-reliance, respect, work and character affirmed by her action.

My parents loved one another in their own way I suppose because,
in the end, ultimately, he understood her suffering she understood his
pain. Their understanding never supplanted the memories of joy and
culture that were visited upon their children.

Today I stand swaying nearer the gates of my ancestors, moving a bit
slower but understanding how the fatigue of fear destroys the fabric,
spirit and beauty of a life, indeed lives. But from time to time whisper
a loving word, celebrate culture and whistle a happy tune going and
coming.

BMV

Foolish Lover Blues

The old man related this story to all who cared to listen: Of all the men she ever knew, he was the only man who laid rough hands upon her so gently that they glorified her body and touched the core of her being, touched her soul. So when she struck the first blow after his cavalier farewell, he turned to look at her in shock, wide eyed, their eyes met.

He stared at her trying to understand, but then his wide eyes narrowed and he smiled. Perhaps for the first time in his life, certainly the last, his perspective on life was clarified, certainly as regards to this woman, no this lady, who had brought him so much joy selflessly. And her eyes at this moment told him unspeakable reality, the hurt, the loss felt by this sudden, irrational end of their affair. Her eyes welling with tears, she struck a second blow. He fell to his knees, tears now welling in his eyes, not out of pain or fear, but a final understanding and sorrow.

His final gesture to her was a smile and a nod. This, a man of respect and distinction, understood, in that instant flash between life and eternity we call death, what his lover always knew in a raw and inexplicable way. Her love was not given to careless caprice, play or fancy. Not given in fear of consequence. He smiled in the wisdom of ages as he slipped over to the other side holding her, she him.

He had experienced true love from a tough human being with a gentle soul not considered worthy of consideration by many. He now knew, at life's finale, she viewed him as no plaything, and she was no toy.

She was convicted promptly by a jury of her peers who barely understood the words of love she spoke. She felt no regret, no anger, no fear but only the physical loss of a man whose spirit would ever abide with her. Her lover who never understood until the end that his rough hands brought a kindness to a woman born into a loveless world, who only sought to keep the love of a foolish man she foolishly loved.

BMV

Tammon Stew

The day wore a kind of heat, that clung to the hours like wet silk. The children of Joseph Johnson Elementary School were indifferent to it. Island children possess the magical ability to be unaware of the temperature, until they grow up, and learn they need more mature things to complain about. For now, they jumped, screamed, and darted in the beating sun, across the black top school yard. They carried news that Jimmy and Pete were up in the tammon tree to all who would hear.

Robbie, Jimmy's brother in the 4th grade could hardly believe his ears, and ran to see, leaving his homework for next period to blow into the wind. He weaved through the congregation of children to get a look. Sure enough, there they were, like young panthers balancing themselves expertly in the branches. Sam played wingman, running helter skelter through the brush, picking up the tammons they shook free from the branches.

He placed them into a pouch he fashioned by holding the bottom of his now filthy t-shirt towards his chest with his left hand. Then, he ferried them up to the concrete barricade separating bush from school. Jimmy and Pete cursed him for letting too many drop and break. He quickly assessed that he was not technically on school grounds. This greatly reduced the risk of punishment for foul language, so Sam let loose a barrage of home grown curse words. The litany inspired further glee and fervor in his schoolmates looking down on them from above. Ms. Lewis, keeping a watchful eye over the chaos fought back laughter as she scolded Sam's brazen tongue.

The tree was back in the bush, down a shallow gully where the edge of the old graveyard, the school yard, and old Mr. Johnson's (the school's namesake) property met. It was a cosmic crossroad, where the children and their surroundings communed and became as one.

Some of the children could see their houses peeking from behind the trees in the hills from here. The fifth grade teacher, Ms. Goodman laid her brother to rest in this very cemetery not even a year past. Mr. Johnson, was a living part of Virgin Islands history the children learned about in their studies. His great grandchildren were among the lot running amok in the schoolyard this very morning.

As the ruckus in the hills met its crescendo, the bell rang. Startled, the children looked at each other, in confusion. Their feral abandon interrupted by the intrusion of the piercing chimes, they turned and looked at Ms. Lewis for direction. It was she, after all, who instigated the whole affair.

She recruited some of the bigger boys to harvest the fruit at the onset of recess. Timothy, suspicious of the supernatural qualities present in fruit growing so near the graveyard, declined the request. Some of the children considered Timothy's wisdom. The tree *was* near the graveyard, and everyone knew that's where the jumbies lived.

Countering the children's logic, Ms. Lewis offered a suggestion that questioned the manhood of the twelve-year old boy. Laughter sailed up into the air like a thousand kites. The coddling of boys was not practiced in the Caribbean in 1982. These were a people who tamed this land, by allowing it to make them strong. Hardened like the boulders the mountains shed after rain storms.

In short time, she had her eager recruits in the three boys toiling below. This was indeed her affair, and the ringing bell meant the jig was up. She get catch. In seconds, some sixty 4th to 6th graders would be storming into their classrooms, pockets full of tammons. They would have to explain how they came upon such bounty. Surely, the nearest tree existed over the barricade and beyond the No Trespassing sign, a place forbidden.

"The three all you, finish what you doing. The rest all you, go to class."

The children cheered as though they had all won top prize at one of the rigged games at Carnival Village. Jimmy, Pete and Sam were free of the academic shackles. Black liberation like the songs on the radio and the murals of African villages on the retaining walls the children marveled at driving with their parents over Raphune Hill.

"Ms. Goodman 'gon be mad! All you getting in trouble!" Lucinda, an infamous detractor from schoolyard shenanigans, informed the boys in the tree. All of eleven, she was absolutely aghast at Ms. Lewis' heresy.

"Don't mind she." Ms. Lewis said sucking her teeth, the gold cap on her tooth flashed as she said it.

The students were fascinated with Ms. Lewis. A Rasta woman originally from St. Lucia, she arrived each morning in a beat up red truck, blasting reggae, not of the tourist variety. She would step out of the truck like royalty, wearing the darkest shades existing on the island. Upon her exit, the truck, would race down the mountain, at a speed multiples of the posted school zone speed limit. She was without doubt, the celebrity staff member of the tiny school sitting high up on Mafolie Hill.

Even in the 80s, Rastas were mythic beings to many who lived in the islands. Particularly to children. Some drove around town in refurbished VW bugs, with the Lion of Judah or art lifted from Bob Marley album covers, airbrushed onto the hoods. They blasted dub-infused sermons from the windows through custom sound systems. Some walked the lonely mountain roads, disappearing with their livestock into the bush, going god knows where. Sam imagined they lived back in the woods, living off the land like the cowboys in the old Westerns dubbed in Spanish that played on the TV station from San Juan they could barely pick up.

Rebecca, an astute fourth-grader informed all who would listen, that Ms. Lewis worked obeah. Her father, an accountant and tent church preacher had told her as much. Patrick said in whispers that he had seen her smoking ganja in a parked car with some man down at Coki Beach. Caught red-eyed, she smiled and waved at him as he walked by.

A rebel. Teacher was a rebel. That was all the children needed to understand to inspire their sense of wonder and awe regarding her. The mainland girls could have their Amelia Earharts and Madame Curies to look up to. They had Ms. Lewis, and would take her 100 times over. Besides, Earhart never landed here.

A full five minutes (which might as well be thirty from a child's perspective) after the bell rang, Ms. Lewis decided she had tempted fate enough, and commanded the boys to wash up and return to class. The affair did cause a minor dust-up among the teachers. Ms. Lewis did a twenty minute bid in the principal's office explaining herself, in a conversation that descended into gossip about the new librarian, and the poor quality of cassava at the grocery stores these past few weeks.

Despite all this, and much to Lucinda's chagrin, the next few days went the same. During recess, Jimmy, Pete and Sam were down in the bush collecting tammons at recess, and late to class. Schoolyard gossip maintained, that Ms. Goodman never scolded them. The ever-astute Rebecca, suspected that Ms. Lewis and Mrs. Goodman were probably in cahoots, sending the boys to pick fruit and eat them all up because they were greedy, and full of wickedness.

On Friday morning, Ms. Lewis was in the cafeteria with the cooks, loud and proud women from down island, who spent the days fussing, laughing and making gourmet meals out of government issued processed meat, local spices and sometimes, ground provisions from the farmers, up the mountain. They helped Ms. Lewis stew all those tammons in the kitchen's huge pots. It sent a bouquet of burnt sugar, cinnamon, ginger, and tammon crawling through the aluminum louvres on the windows of the classrooms, distracting the children from mid-morning lessons.

That afternoon during lunch, the cooks dropped a generous dollop of stew tammon on each child's tray. The three teachers from the mainland thanked the cooks kindly, but dared not eat. Who could say what was in the strange paste? Was it sanitary? Legal? But the kids, island-born and stateside transplants alike, devoured their portions greedily. Even Timothy had reasoned, any jumbie residing in the fruit, would surely have been exorcised by the boiling water, and the watchful eye of Jesus.

It was made clear to the students that the tammon came from their own labor. Jimmy, Pete and Sam were even called in to the principal's office and commended for their work. Each was given a small glass jar of stewed tammon to take home as payment for their labor. The jars made it home in various degrees of emptiness.

As they grew older, many of the children would move to the mainland. They would remember school yard pig roasts on Friday nights when the parents would share food, and drink together, while the children played in the schoolyard to the music of coqui and crickets. They would smile recalling times the errant stray goat would wander from the bush into the yard. They would remember a time, when life was sweet like tammon stew, and the sun, a competent alchemist, would rise each morning to test new hues of gold and red in the secrecy of the dawn-lit sky.

DJV

Old Griot

There once lived a self-proclaimed prince on the Isle of Joy and Warmth. The Prince was arrogant. The people of the Isle knew he and his ministerial minions thought less of them than their lap cats. But, the people believed the Prince needed them more than they needed him. At least so they thought. In time the people became complacent. Steeped in the history of the past, but fearful of the future and living solely for the here and now, the citizenry, forgetting their ancient past and survival craft, became enticed by the ease of vice, lust and folly. The Prince became addicted to gluttony, graft and greed. But in time children cried, adults died, and the Isle lost its pride. And sprits of the ancestors moaned and wept in the depths of the timeless sea where neither cry was heard nor tears observed.

And it came to pass that this Prince of Arrogance, now thought to be a Prince of Fools, and the people of the Isle realized they had lost their identity. It was only then that the progeny of an ancient tribe, well known by their smile, came with a selfish plan in mind. While the people of the Isle worked and frolicked by day, the progeny of the ancient tribe plotted by night. And in time the elders of the Isle of Joy and Warmth passed from life, the youth moved elsewhere in frustration, or lost their freedom in houses of thick walls and iron gates. Leaderless and without a plan, the people of the once joyous Isle began to lose their land which made them powerless indeed. The Isle's practiced living without a clue, led the progeny of the ancient tribe to take pride in the planned bloodless coup. Who can be blamed? Who can be sued, when people are complicit in their own ruin.

But unexpectedly, out of the gloom, there rose young citizens from the Projects of Hope. Simple the action, scope and plan, 'leh we take back we pride, 'leh we take back we land. The elders of lost pride asked how could this ever come true. The youth of Hope simply responded, "What would you do for the Isle's survival, for a revolution anew?" And, the spirit of ancestors so often ignored, woke to the question, for the answer they knew, and whispered silently, whispered true, survival lies not only in ideas, but in willingness to take action, the willingness to do.

As the old storyteller rose, ready to go, he spied a young boy sitting in the dust, beating out a rhythmic tune on his knees. Dressed in tattered but clean white and black clothes, the child seemed to be sending out a prayer on a Bata Drum as if he were the mighty Shango calling upon wise Elegua, there at the crossroads of the Isle, to come help his people choose the proper path. The old Griot smiled at the young drummer with understanding and wisdom of the of the ages. He said to the people of the Isle before he left, "We live in a cauldron of stew not yet blend, cric' crac', the wheel may turn, but we story never end."

BMV

* Both Elegua, (also referred to as Elegba), and Shango are Orishas (deities) in both the traditional Yoruba, and Santería religions. Elegua is described as a gatekeeper found at the crossroad between humanity and the divine. He is an Orisha with the distinction of being both an Orisha and Ajogun. Orishas and Ajoguns can be viewed similarly as angels and demons respectively, in the Western cultural sense. The historic Shango was the third Oyo (ruler) of the Oyo Kingdom (Yoruba Empire), while the deified Shango can be described as the god of thunder and lightning in these religious traditions.

J and B

A Georgia gentleman. Calm and cool.
Carolina beauty. Reserved with charm.

Brave as lions they had to be
citizens of color traveling, fearful not quite "free"
in search of a loveland
in search of dignity.

Eponymous symbols of
Africa's many
swept up in a nation's greed,
it's manifest destiny.

Who knows what gentle minds conceal
in an onslaught of relentless misery
caused by their own country.
A people oppressed in a time of depression.

But in hidden spaces some nights
when Dexter blew and Eckstein crooned,
a cool black man swayed,
a charmed woman wooed.

I sat at times
digging on old joyous blues
sipping scotch with him and breaking bread with the two
carefully listening to what their silence said, looking for clues.

Not spoken as yet
but certainly true
they were progeny of the best warriors the world ever knew.
Survivors of a blood thirsty brood.

Yes, shape shifting Africans
still on the lam
evading the Empire of Eagle's claws and beaks
with logic, invisibility, sometimes grace and mystique.

I now see these old warriors
In a different way.
They braved the darkness
and welcomed the day

Ah! I sense your mind working.
What's that you said?
Whiskey working all up in my head
and my words don't rhyme like good poetry should.

Not to be unkind
but I differ with you.
Poetry needs no rhythm or rhyme
It simply needs reason and needs to be true.

BMV

Reign of Fiyah

Fiyah next time
Is what churchman dem say
But 'tis wind and rain
Mash up meh home.

Fiyah nah have chance to bun'.

But meh children dem call me
Tell me and say
ragamuffin klan and
supremacist dem on parade.

What a melee!

KKK and baldhead man
mash up the city
torch in dem han'
say racist history is dem culture.

Dem nah cyare who hear.

Police stand by and
twiddle dem thumbs
'til young girl get kill,
man beat to the grung.

President actions say is way it should be.

I tell meh children
who smarter than me
'tis time to come home.
President nah cyare 'bout you, 'bout we.

Buh dem say back strong
and 'bout freedom to speak.

I's a poor old man.
I may not be bright
but I know right to bear arms
Trumps First Amendment right.*

Meh guess the reign of fiyah come.
Is it time we consider pick up de gun?

BMV

*Publisher's Note: (The author is aware the right to bear arms is the Second
Amendment of the United States Constitution)

100 Cities

There were 100
teeming with life
black faces in numbers
shaming the untold sum of creation
hurling through the violent cosmos
exposing their undying light in cosmic pageantry

the Dogon knew

100 with streets weaving across the land
connecting souls with laughter
in tongues born
from the honey of Earth
the sediment and dust of all things before them
fallen down to the floor of her bosom
the soil thriving
granting and taking life

100
Benin City, walls stretching
lengths farther than cares
dug into the earth in thunder
by the Edo
expanding
majestic

fabric the colors of wild dagga
water hyacinth

and devils thorn
draped around the dreams of stone carved black and brown children
cool water and sky
to soothe the aching cries woven
into the curtains of inhumanity
drawing upon them

Kumasi and Chinguetti and Walata, and Timbuktu
where some, have said 3,000 ancient tomes
handwritten in the drift of cloud lifted voices
of the Mande and the Fulani, the Sudani
exist, untouched by modern scholars
skins parched for sun and truth
liars kneeling to the hornets
feasting on their eyes
buzzing gray patterns
in closed thoughts
tunnel visions
and silos
funnels
clogged with the muck of distorted light
the milk of scholars
curdled at the breast
a fitting meal for denizens
of confusion
romantic in their flight
Amazed at Pythagoras and not his teachers
sitting in halls of Diospolis in Egypt
where the fool was bathed from his heart
his garb of dead animal skins stripped from his body

before he was let to enter the temple

There were 100
cities bursting with joyful song
mournful souls
beggars and kings
singers and lovers
children and godlings
thieves and scholars at the gates
to the wilderness of Eden

Kilwa in Tanzania
rising in the 9th century
carved by black hands
that carved your highways
slathering them with black pitch
and time served

in Africa
laying her castles gently at the ocean's lips
trading with lands thought legend
burned by the Portuguese
bringing small pox like flowers
each pedal a hallowed death
grinding lives to a suffering halt
hailed in shades of panic
crossed from the book of names

There were 100
Mombasa and Vaida

kings with gold around their necks
long before hemp rope
lemonade and county fairs

Amina Queen of Nigeria
Nzinga Queen of Angola

untouched by the sting of the whip
their honor preserved

bow before you

there were 100 cities
burning
crumbling
the marrow of bones
blackened from soot
churning into a slurry of terror

100 cities
African and proud
snuffed from the light
by a thirst for something
better than the cold
scurvy and open sores
drifting on tyrannical seas

blighted leaves on vines of black splendor

there were 100 cities

and they are gone
brought to heel and scattered
by the gentle
Sunday morning haze

DJV

** This poem was inspired by a historical essay entitled "100 Cities Destroyed By Europeans" by Mawuna Koutonin.

The poem was originally published in English/French Literary journal, Post: Blank by Mad Gleam Press.

Irony

I listen teacher
from New Yawk
come tell we children
how to talk

How to use verbs "is" and "are"
and how to elaborate ending suffix "ing" so it not sound like "in"
but a hardy ending like the glorious "ing" in sing
and not the horrid "in" in sin

The children giggled, and oohed in delight

Buh I wondered to myself
who this woman from afar come teach we
Sounds like she come
Make fun ah we

I sure she nah waste time
telling New Yawker dem how to speak English tongue.
She should be shame
She cyan speak like West Indian

Shame nah help we speak, read or write!

I wanted to know, seemed puzzling to me
since nearly every sentence she spoke
began with word "so"
So I akse her the question and her face come like snow

She say it's modern vernacular.
So, like "in" nah "ing", smilin' I tell she
Buh teacher face come hard and then she ask
Bwoy why yuh so rude? Why yuh so fass'?

Only now children start giggle, ooh and laugh
while teacher face come look just like ash
Buh a happy thought come over me
as teacher now learning to talk just like we

BMV

Even Now

The soft hours that hover near dawn are a borderland to reality. Our morning rituals reel us fully into the fold. Alarm clocks callously pry us from our dreams. The wrapping of children in school uniforms, dumping a spoonful of freeze dried coffee into hot water, microwaving packets of oatmeal are spells that roust us to our waking life. Even now, in 2056, the rituals had not changed much, in St. Thomas.

Sitting on the edge of his bed, Danny Baptiste began his morning ritual. He didn't own an alarm clock. His body was attuned to the sun, the final bow of the crickets, and the rooster's crow. Danny rose each day with the ability to see each one as a new canvas. It was an enviable skill, and he was a living wellspring of hope here on the Northside.

By 6:30 AM, he would stand on the porch, freshly showered and barefoot, sipping bush tea and taking in the beauty of Hull Bay, way down the mountain. With his binoculars, he could see the dinghies make their way through the water, manned by the last of the fishermen bringing in their morning haul. The pelicans nearby, would be jealous of their bounty. Pelicans always unsettled him. They seemed to stare through you as they bobbed in the calm pulse of the bay, reading your secrets.

His grandfather tried relentlessly, to teach him how to build and tend to lobster traps on Hull Bay as a youth. Danny couldn't be bothered with such things. Some of the "old ways" had lost the battle for the cultural psyche of these islands long ago. Even the coqui appeared to sing a different song than the one he remembered as a child. The idea of spending a life harvesting lobster and selling them to the hotels for a pittance seemed insulting to him.

His grandfather would shake his head, telling him, "I ain' tryin' to teach you to make money, boy. I tryin' teach you to how to stay alive."

Hopeful though he was, Danny was also a little thick, and so his grandfather's words never bloomed into the gardens they might have become. Humility was a depleted currency in the new world. Globalization was an economic mudslide, for small islands lacking large quantities of resources that could be exploited. They had nothing to be packaged and sold in mass. There was constant fear that every pay check might be the last. Every month, more people left to the mainland, though things weren't much better there these days. The sense of dwindling economic futures had rendered humility a luxury. Today it was dog eat dog...cat...mouse, and all, it seemed.

Danny worked for a distant cousin's shipping company loading containers onto barges, and avoided two rounds of downsizing. He'd probably dodge another. You kept an eye on family ferociously here, no matter how distant the kin. His brother Joey, asleep down the hall, lost two shifts at Food Plus, keeping him close to home. Belts were tightening. Fortunately for the brothers, they lived in the tiny one story concrete slab of a home their Grandfather left them.

He pleaded with the brothers never to sell it. It was their legacy. Their buffer against the tyranny of the world. As long as they could make the property tax, they had a place to stay nobody could ever take away from them. So far, by the Lord's grace, they made it work.

By 6:50 AM, like clockwork, he was in his rust mauled 4x4 pushing up a steep, barely-present road hewn from potholes like moon craters, and matted down short grass. The taller guinea grass served the purpose of creating blind spots. The road was paved once. But the elements do not play fair, and now it looked as though it may well have been, not a road, but a foot path used by the ancients who hauled cane up the steep inclines to make rum for the Europeans.

Danny thought rum was the best thing the Europeans left behind when they tired of playing safari and went back across the ocean, leaving their former captives to fend for themselves. Through hundreds of years of adversity, those captives, now a free people, knew triumph. Adversity was just another song, and the people sang through each verse with effortless joy.

He laughed at himself for having rum on the mind so early in the morning, but Easter was almost here. That meant Carnival was around the corner. During masse, the contemplation of rum was acceptable at any time of the day. There would be time enough to fire a few with his friends and family in the weeks ahead.

Carnival could be said to be the revelation of a Virgin Islander's true self, but also the true state of the community's living soul. His Caribbean History professor at UVI once suggested, in jest, that Carnival is the biggest religion on the island. In particular Danny looked forward to Calypso Tent this year. Local officials had carried on in ways to make the seediest of the fallen angels, blush. This year's low hanging fruit was abundant, and so were the Calypsonians.

"Dumb Bread and Cheese" By The Mighty Spear had been blasting out of car windows, and at the wooden shed bars where the local men sat on benches near coal pots, frying fish, and slamming dominoes on tables as though the chunks of plastic meant them harm. The song detailed an alleged incident whereupon the Commissioner of Finance was found in a compromising position afterhours in his office, when the cleaning man barged in thinking it unoccupied.

Danny chuckled to himself singing, "Who is the dumb bread? Who is the cheese?" His pitchy vibrato filled the 4x4 with mirth. His silver capped tooth shone as he laughed.

Scandals, for the most part, in the Virgin Islands were usually in good fun, at the end of the day. Men and women who had tumbled to the bottom with a heart crushing thud, could always claw their way back in this community. You may have to suffer years of good natured ribbing, but you were never cast out. Your humanity was never forgotten. Redemption is woven into the psyche of the societies dreamed and built by the daughters and sons of slaves. Wherever in the world they exist. It is the perfect fifth, that guides their song of freedom.

The 4x4 panted as it reached the lip of St. Peter Mountain Road, a well-paved street, mostly. It wound like a blacktop river through the hills. Just past the pass up to Crown Mountain, he turned down the steep, barely visible road leading down to Scott Free. There were better paved roads to get to the airport, but this way, he could pass Sheila's house. Sometimes he'd catch her leaving to go to work herself. He would hail her up, waving through the window leaned back in the driver's seat like the guys in music videos. She was going with a mechanic who had a shop in Soto Town, but people's realities change every day. No harm planting himself in the corners of her mind.

When he reached the new parking lot at the airport, he got out of the truck and stretched. He wiped a layer of sweat from his brow, with the washcloth he carried around for just that purpose. He waved to his co-workers drinking coffee and eating breakfast on the far side of the lot. He then made his way over to the aluminum sided food truck parked right outside the lot. His morning ritual didn't finish until he put a Johnny cake in his waist, and said good morning to Ms. Ann.

"Ms. Ann, you save me one or 'wha?" Danny's voice arrived at the food truck before he did, and he heard her sucking her teeth in response before he could see her.

"Boy, the 'ting sell off."

"'Wha, you ain't hold me one?" His disappointment wore a tone of mockery. Ms. Ann was the den mother to the few dozen workmen who gathered here every day. She filled them with coffee in the morning, and cold beers when they made their way home. She knew everything about everybody that passed through that parking lot.

Ms. Ann sucked her teeth again, and shuffled over to the stove on the right of the truck. She opened the lid of a pot, and a thick aroma like butter, thyme, earth, and sea escaped through the steam. She picked up a small plastic container, and using a long stainless steel spoon, filled it. She poked a plastic fork in the center and rudely shoved it in his waiting hands.

"Taste this for me."

He inspected the tiny mountain of food before him. "Ms. Ann, you're the best."

She asked for nothing, but he punched a generous sum into his device and transferred the payment to her, before turning around to join his co-workers.

"Don't tell them where you get it. All of dem 'gon harass me."

"We safe, Ms. Ann." He smiled and went on his way.

The comment was made in jest. Hers was the only place to get food in this part of town. The bacteria and algae cluttering coastlines and beachfronts had brought with it health risks, and a rancid smell few could tolerate. The marine biologists at UVI said it would all pass, but that was months ago. Many shops and restaurants nearest the sea, simply waved the white flag, and boarded up. The mosquitos stayed.

Through the fence at the edge of the parking lot, Danny stared at the ruins of Pelican Reef. The water was above the ankles now, in what used to be an outdoor patio restaurant. Pelican Reef was a budget beachside hotel built in the 1960s, rebuilt in the 1990s after

Marilyn ravaged the coast, again after the storms of 2017, and one last time late in the 2020s.

After the storms of 2043, it was left a ruin. In fact, some quick-thinking American film students shot a hit indie horror in the corridors of the sinking hotel a few years ago. Danny's attention turned to his co-workers who were getting in their morning gossip. In the distance, the company trucks were barreling down the partially submerged road towards them.

The Airport, was no longer an airport. Planes hadn't landed there in years. But, it was a good enough staging ground for the barges to head out to the cargo ships anchored off shore, and ferry goods to trucks that could pass the sunken coastal roads. The barges made use of docks fashioned from lumber and the concrete bones of the old runway. The locals still called it The Airport because, why not?

It would be years before the docks at Havensight and Crown Bay would be rebuilt. Waterfront was all but washed out. But, the people needed goods. Makeshift harbors were an interim solution that had been in operation for the past two years.

When the trucks pulled up, Danny and the small crew he worked with, boarded the same one. The men strapped into their seats like soldiers in a state of the art military transport vehicle. In fact, they were converted military transports. Surplus from one of America's newer wars. Before strapping in himself, Danny went to work on his food before the truck pulled out and scattered it everywhere. He ate greedily, drawing the attention of Robbie, whose own stomach was grumbling.

"What you eating?" Robbie asked.

"Whelks and rice." Danny said, matter-of-factly, with a full mouth, not bothering to meet his gaze.

"Where you get that from?"

"How you mean?" Danny responded. The phrase had a thousand meanings in the Virgin Islands, yet each Virgin Islander could detect which you meant, through employing a complex cadence analysis algorithm innate to the species.

"Ms. Ann give you that?" Robbie insisted, pursuing his inquiry to its needless and obvious end.

Robbie sucked his teeth slowly in mock disgust. Danny smiled and the men laughed. When the container was 2/3 gone, he handed it to Robbie, who made quick work of the rest. The food had evaporated by the time the driver cut the engine on. Minutes later, the truck splashed through the last stretch of sunken road, having hit the hard bump that always made it seem as though they were about to dive into a watery oblivion.

When the truck stopped, the men began to fasten their hardhats. The men got out and walked toward the barge tethered to the landing. Before boarding, Danny shielded his eyes, making his hands a visor, and looked into the blue sky. Soon, they were a few hundred yards out, maneuvering the barge underneath the crane of a ship filled with shipping containers.

Danny and his co-workers sat inside the control units maneuvering the hydraulic arms of the 'bots'. These were not the high tech anime-styled things, controlled by some willful AI, as the dystopians imagined. They were fully articulate arms of titanium and polycarbonate, extending from a dull grey hub. They looked like huge tin mint boxes with robotic arms capable of lifting 6,000 lbs. They were fixed to bases that ran a grid of tracks on the barge's main deck. The men would send them zipping back and forth, loading containers onto the barge.

They spent the remainder of the day yelling at one another from across their control posts. Their laughter offended the severity of their socio-economic reality. The happiness that comes with ignoring one's social class, is a transcendence more spiritual than many will ever know. At the very least, it allowed for vibrant lives to resonate joyously in the green mountains that stretched their necks up and towards the sun, from the blue mirror that is sea.

After a time, there was a round of downsizing even Danny couldn't escape. But, he found that it didn't matter much to him. A few months back, out of boredom, or perhaps fruit from the garden of memories about his grandfather, he began building lobster traps. And in time, he would push his same rust withered shell of a 4x4 down to Hull Bay. He would leave it where the road stopped and the new water's edge began. He and his cousins would go out every day at 5AM checking and setting the traps, before the morning sun sent so much as a flare into the sky.

On Sundays, they would sit in the hills on Danny's balcony and eat lobster right off the grill, and of course sip rum. Sheila would make a butter sauce with garlic, thyme and a pinch of scotch bonnet from right out the garden. Joey would play a guitar, and they would sing.

The hills sparkled with candles, lanterns and outdoor cooking fires like fairy lights. The air was alive with the hum of generators, laughter and song. They were forgotten Americans caught in an eternal limbo dance beneath the poverty line. Victims of excess and the world's shiny new climate. Still, they lived, and loved the joy of life, like royals of a forgotten bloodline. Even now, thriving in the shadows of distress.

DJV

Cradle

I,
The prodigal one,
Who traveled countless miles in search of self
Who left warm sun for northern skies and
Chilly smiles of customs unknown

Awakened now I return to the island cradle of my being and essence
of my soul

I search for the love left behind
Absurdly believing she awaits my return
Though I know she has had many others
Before and after me

And yet there she is
Serenely seated on her coastal throne
She undulates in blue
Flecks of yellow gold dust twinkle in her eyes
She notices me and smiles

Wistfully she comes my way
Fragrances of passion fruit and jasmine fill the air
Can it be she recognizes me
My avatar of beauty and countless dreams
Calmly embraces the whole of me like a gentle breeze

I sink into her liquid arms
Trying to embrace her warmth, her beauty, her charm

But how does one grasp the wind
How does one grip the sea

I lay wet, languidly floating in her embrace
My senses awake to her siren song
She whispers seductively:
I am the eternal temptress of the sea
Here for you and all who see

Before Columbus I guided vessels of Abu Bakar II
Ushered Caribs and Arawaks to many islands of my sea

Whimsiccally crushed conquistadors and slavers for their greed
Sustained ancestors in their dire time of need
And I bring you to me

I am a great reservoir of life and warmth
No matter how harshly the sea rages or the winds may blow
I am the sacred keeper of secrets and your ancestral bones
I am to be honored, never owned
Though far you have traveled
And far have you roamed
The Caribbean is your harbor
Your refuge
and home

BMV

The King's Storyteller

Pirate king
resting on throne
of woven palms
sitting in the folds
of a kapok tree

the tigers curled around
his mud caked boots
are shadow

On Saturdays
after morning rains
I would visit him
sliding down the gut
below the spring
of Spring Road

slipping and jumping
over stones
fingers finding the spaces
between the thorns
of the monkey no climb tree
for balance
stepping over
streams of rain water
cascading violently down
the mountain

a frequent traveler
of this road
I knew where the patches
of catch and keep
lay in hiding
to tear at exposed flesh
grab at the fabric
of clothes
now filthy with
mountain
but
the rain would
make
nests of red ants
invisible

a phantom danger

one that could turn
real
sending younglings
into fits of screaming
in the bush
where mother could not hear

nature teaching children
life lessons
tears welling in eyes
a price paid
to meet the king

mongoose
feral cat
stray dog
lizard
weaving through
the green
invisible
rustling the leaves
inspiring feigned fear
a purse of imagination
full and overflowing
the wealth of a child
is not measured in silver

In the heartland
lay the temporary pools
where root
rock stone
and mud
created cauldrons
used by cane toad
to rear their young

hands filthy with mud
wiped clean on the sides of jeans
that came from the laundromat
just yesterday

The plastic men

hiding in pockets
now air dropped
to the rocky shores

plastic weapons
wedged into their hands

the fury of battle whispered
into their blank stares

slogging through the water
to find the enemy

hiding behind the rocks

the battles were legendary
triumph and tyranny
unfolding like red velvet curtains
of the theaters in the old world

stories fit for a pirate king
and the tigers are shadow

DJV

The Brothers

Two brothers of the skin, perhaps of blood, meet and greet the other with the strength of friendship born of common experience. They slap palms so strongly, and embrace so warmly, that some passersby scatter left and right. The sinister power of the dap and respect.

It's evening, caution time in the city where masses hastily retreat to segregated enclaves. But these men meet oblivious of suspect stares and fear they might engender. Hardened men, once children of the street, greet one another letting their involuntary tension and defenses take a holiday. Grimace replaced by smiles normally hidden from the world outside their doors. These men made rigid by everyday tension, oppression, depression salute each other as men of old because intuitively they know they are the children of the first but this may be the last time they greet. They sought out a table where, for some precious moments, they could sort out the rough and tumble of their lives and their improbable survival in the journey beyond their teenage years.

The rotating bar offered a 360 degree night skyline view of the city, vistas they never expected as youths but which they aspired to nonetheless. And yet here they were – an elite of the gully and one of the polite urbs – heartily laughing about their young lives as the feared ones, and also the frightened. Laughing at the prospect that they may both be gentrified out of their homes. The children of white flight were returning with a vengeance and bringing with them their guardians, gun slingers, sons of thunder, the city's blue blaze terrors.

Ironically, the two men's survival made them see the richness of their experience. They talked of pilfered empty soda bottles from the bottle plant so they could get up enough money to go to the movie matinee and buy movie house popcorn. The best! They reminisced about the liquid soft queens who they made out with in the stairwells of the projects and how they never really appreciated their beauty until it was a time too late. They spoke of their first and present loves, broken hearts and pride in their children. Their eyes clouded over when the memory turned to injury, jail, subjects of mayhem and all too early death, matters that came up when the question was raised: whatever happened to ...? or, Do you ever hear from ...? Momentary silence fell as the men considered good and bad fortune that followed when they took different paths at their personal crossroads. Two men speaking like any two men could except their character was so profoundly etched by color and the socio-economic realities that followed.

It was getting late now. Night had fallen. An edgy time in the city. A time to retreat to their world. They had drunk finely and dined on gourmet appetizers, and enjoyed the recollection of friendship born of hard knock days. Though they had every reason to smile in honor of the joy this meeting of souls brought, it was time to hit the road to their actual or figurative walled in world, though in the same city. A city not always welcoming to their style and hue. They had to enter a landscape where their defenses would once again become alert, gentleness set aside, and enter a place where villain and protector can be foe. Their smiles started to wane, hearts began to harden, parting became a bit more abstract with hints of pessimism as they clasped hands and hugged one another as strong men can, hoping to see one another again but never certain. They had a distance to travel, two brothers living in places within a nation apart, always trekking a precarious path. They knew that between sunrise and the moon, between the hustle and flow, trouble was never far from their door. But at the crossroads where they parted ways so many years ago, they were of a single mind – they prepared themselves for moments of blues, however, they never expect to lose.

Snow was falling now. Soon slush would follow. They had to go their way. Cold snow would soon cover them if allowed. They had to find warmth of love. They had to find light of love. They had to find their way home

BMV

Flowers and Lead Vases

Pregnant Spring full of promise
Bountiful Summer
Elegant leaves, colorful, begin to Fall
And wither in the cold only to bring forth life again.
But
Old men of Winter,
Hearts of snow,
Send forth beautiful, budding flowers
In lead vases
That often fall heavily
And poison the ground
Scattering frenzied masses to far off spaces
Only to find other men of Winter,
Civilized barbarians,
Who caused frigid snow to fall
Upon nature's beauty
Upon its elegance
Upon the dust of life.
Now void of the natural order of things
Warm hearts wonder in flight
Will Winter chill give way to
Spring's promise of new life and
Fulgent Summer's warm, nurturing light,
or will
Fall's colorful growth and seeds of life
Crumble beneath the cold, white snow, and
Wither to speckles that give life no more,
The result of poisonous lead vases.

BMV

Father & Sun

When the cosmos was cold and uncaring
burning purple with hunger and beauty
And the ripples of time but infants
To those there to perceive
Raced to carve all destinies

The father born
Of mother's invention
Sat in the cool rays
Of the novas birthing
In the cauldron
For thousands of years
Before even the years
Were born

In one he saw a silver tear of joy
Floating in its core

He knelt at the edge and plucked it
From the wellspring of creation

He placed it in a patch
Of black sky
To warm it's ebon bones

He sang to him a song
He had learned from the echoes
Of celestial gowns blowing

Between the galaxies

What am I?
the young Star asked

Sun
Said the father

What will I do?
Asked the sun
Shine your soul into breath
He replied

What if I fail
He asked

You will
the father replied

What will I do then
asked the sun

Shine
Said the father

DJV
(For my father)

The Authors

Bernard M. VanSluytman, was born in British Guyana (now Guyana), and grew up in Brooklyn, New York. He studied at Howard University Law School, and moved with his family to St. Thomas in 1974. There he served in the VI Office of Attorney General under Hon. Judge Verne A. Hodge, engaged in his private practice of law for 26 years, and for three years served as Solicitor General of the VI under Hon. John de Jongh, Jr., Governor, and Hon. Vincent Fraser, Attorney General, until his retirement in 2015. He is married to retired VI Public School teacher, Gail Davis VanSluytman.

Darius Jamal VanSluytman is his son. He is a writer, electronic musician and producer. His work with various groups earned him critical acclaim from SPIN, Pitchfork, MTV and overseas editions of Vogue and Rolling Stone. He's performed at The Whitney Museum, The Frist Museum, The Kitchen, the SONAR Festival in Barcelona, and Il Teatro Manzoni in Milan. Most recently he performed original work at the Frist Museum in Nashville (2018). He has appeared in alternative theater performances in the United States and abroad, and the feature film *Lifted* (2010). His first professional published work appeared in The Virgin Islands Daily News.

AN ADMONITION FOR THE VIRGIN ISLANDS

A VI Proverb admonishes: "cockroach have no business in fowl house." A poignant observation on many levels of animal, and more importantly, human relationships. I invite your attention to an African proverb, Ibo I believe. It goes something like this: "If the cockroach wishes to rule the chicken, it must first hire the fox as a bodyguard."

Admonition: Beware the cockroach and the fox!

For Beth (1947 – 2018) Where you fly we will follow...where you land we will find... for after a time there is another time...

www.ingramcontent.com/pod-product-compliance
Lightning Source LLC
Chambersburg PA
CBHW030544200626
46812CB00020BA/1810